THE WHITE LIGHT OF TOMORROW

The White Light *of* Tomorrow

RUSSELL THORNTON

poems

The White Light *of* Tomorrow

RUSSELL THORNTON

HARBOUR PUBLISHING

Harbour Publishing Co. Ltd.
P.O. Box 219, Madeira Park, BC, VON 2H0
www.harbourpublishing.com

Edited by Silas White
Cover image by neonnspb / Adobe Stock
Cover design by Libris Simas Ferraz / Onça Design
Text design by Carleton Wilson
Printed and bound in Canada
Printed on 100% recycled paper

Supported by the Province of British Columbia

Harbour Publishing acknowledges the support of the Canada Council for the Arts, the Government of Canada, and the Province of British Columbia through the BC Arts Council.

LIBRARY AND ARCHIVES CANADA CATALOGUING IN PUBLICATION
Title: The white light of tomorrow / Russell Thornton.
Names: Thornton, Russell, author.
Identifiers: Canadiana (print) 20230447880 | Canadiana (ebook) 20230447902 |
    ISBN 9781990776533 (softcover) | ISBN 9781990776540 (EPUB)
Classification: LCC PS8589.H565 W55 2023 | DDC C811/.54—dc23

Contents

IV

I

A Sheet Metal Sink

No one knew I found a large lidless box
made of sheet metal to serve as a sink,
set it on a low bench next to my bed,
filled it with water I carried in pots
from an outside tap. Nightly the water
became more and more deeply still, and dark.
Then in the morning, when I put my hands
in the water, it generated sparks.
When I cupped it, lifted it eye-level,
the water bristled with white light and caught
like pure electricity at my skin.
There where I stayed below ground in an old
basement with a dirt floor, I felt afraid,
but daily after school I emptied the sink,
later filled it according to my wish
to be completely alone. The water
lay in the random metal container
while I slept, and when I had stood, held it,
and it turned fiery though it was cold,
I saw water secretly watching me
from everywhere. When I had measured it
in my sink, I had brought all water close.
When I washed my face, I founded my own
aloneness, and then when I was no one,
waked within the aloneness of water.

The Sea Wolf in the Stone

I

A rocky hill covered with a stand of tall trees
overlooking the meeting of a river and a sea.
Sunlight falls through the great floating branches
into a clearing to the sandstone earth,
the rays a single rough crystal of quietness.
Worlds of green thickets, fronds and primordial moss
hold up the light that made them to the sun.

II

I parked in the highway pullout. No one was here
except a ragged man, hat brim hiding his eyes,
taking a piss beyond the park sign near a tree.
I thought I would walk past at a distance,
then I looked again, and he was gone. The pathway
swept up and around in a long curve. I could hear
the highway traffic through the gathering
of cedar, fir, maple, arbutus and elm. I came to a cave,
a black recess within a rise of enormous boulders,
went in and for some reason listed for myself
the dirty blankets, food wrappers, backpack,
scattered needles. A short way off, saw the wire fence
separating the place from private property,
houses with a view of the water and city harbour.

III

What do my eyes need? To see the quick waft
and a curving of space stir the branches
before I can say it is a bird and recall its name,
wings spiralling the lit motes of the air. The breeze
swirling leaves for me to follow to where they come to rest
and disintegrate in the dark in the chapels
of the crannies in the rock. What do my hands need
except to touch what I am not? Water declares
it is to drink, berries announce they are to eat,
and fish reveal I must trust the long tracks
they make through the sea's glooms, the surprises of sun.
Light and rock meet, and rock flows like water
through designs it finds and loses again.

IV

On the way here I saw a small street-corner bar,
old wood facade, old neon sign in the window,
and stopped and briefly thought I would go in.
Nanaimo, Vancouver, London, New York…
In the sun-haze, sewage smell, tanker spill,
whale-killing cruise ship roar and effluent
up and down the Salish Sea. Concrete of sidewalks
filled with people lying flat and asphalt of back alleys
beckoned like beautiful substances, couches of true gods.

V

If I could come upon a clear carving
lit within a close circle of trees, I might stretch
my sight across the sandstone and surrounding earth.
Lie face down, reach, and hold with my fingers
to where the earth poured out cold, bright-dark energy
allowing me to fulfill the flow of my death.
A carving might outline me here in my moment
of attendant trees and sunlight and stone
suspended in a river ripple, a sea wave.

VI

I think of the temperature in my locked car
in the season's aberrant extreme heat.
And of my fingers on the handwheel of a metal lathe
in a factory shop my father's father owned. My job
is to turn the metal stock to the proper two-thousandths
of an inch to make a small machine part,
all the time applying cutting fluid
to lubricate and cool the lathe tool and metal shavings.

VII

I am flesh, blood and bone, yet I am living air
moving apart from myself along the leaf-layered ground,
then along the interface where carvings appear.
Here is a diagram created in trance-swirls
with a carving tool a thousand, two thousand years ago.
A large-eyed, whale-finned wolf with raised back hair,
huge lolling tongue, undulating parallel lines for ribs,
its form a fluid energetic curve.

VIII

The sea wolf, the other creatures I begin to make out,
all depicted according to a code,
are all the work of a single individual,
his signature drawn in the strict flow of his line.
His human self-portrait is a carving nearby
of a figure in a radiating headdress,
his own code face with eyes all black pupil,
the details of his skeleton visible like an x-ray.

IX

The creature half-wolf, half-whale hunting
across the sea is his other self-portrait. The sea wolf
pursues its sustenance, and he pursues
the invisible to where he forms it,
hunts beginnings to where he ends. His pulse
echoes in the pulse he records with his travelling hand.

X

The touch of water, which is light. The touch
of the day and all days. Water directing me
to the endless gaze of the carver carrying
likenesses across distances greater
than can be imagined in any need, continuing
in the brightening clearing, pictures forming in the air
between the trees and arriving unknown in stone.

Petroglyph Park, Nanaimo

Description

Turn, oh Shulamite…
—Song of Songs 7:1

If you turn, and I say what I see as you turn,
I must say it in the presence of death, and meet my life in an elsewhere—

while light draws itself around you, and is a sheer garment,
and multiple pairs of small singing birds perch in the swaying folds

of that garment, which burns yet does not expire;
the birds undress themselves of their feathers—they are invisible.

If you turn, you appear, you at once disappear—
you dance to the heartbeat of all yesterdays and tomorrows.

Along a fiery, rising wave, seabirds spiral and cry their one note;
along glittering river ripples and around a river mouth

they follow a stitching intricate and vast, and forever incomplete.
If you turn, the more you express, the more you leave unexpressed;

your garment burns with grief that is alive.
The glance of your eye, the spinning circle of your navel—

I wait as you walk down a wedding aisle of time, or as you circle me
under a canopy, where the glass of all matter will shatter underfoot.

If I name you, I must name the empty space in my cells,
and if my eyes trace you, I am blind as ash, as you dance.

Galleries

The locks of your head are like purple;
a king is held captive in the galleries.
—Song of Songs 7:6

In a distant city, I waited where we had agreed to meet
but you did not appear. Then I saw the sweep and the swerve

of your hair and I began following along a narrow street
that opened on another street, and another, until

I was lost in darkening shadow where the stone
of the winding alleyways had hidden people from the hot sun

for as long as memory had wound through anyone.
Here you could look up, eyes led along angled stone,

and view an eclipse of the sun, streets revealing phases.
I walked farther and farther, with unaided eyes.

To discern a single strand of your hair
would be to view the total phase of a total solar eclipse.

To turn and find you would be to face a blind spot,
an expanding black dot, a blindness that was sight.

The city would be traced by the moon's umbra. The moon
would occult the sun as during the first eclipse. The light

would open before me. I would see your hair—
it would lead me and there would be no way back.

Moon

Thy navel is like a round goblet,
which wanteth not liquor.
—Song of Songs 7:3

There are couplets that evade translation
over and over down through the millennia,

and immortals who take multiple names.
There is your name, "moon" in one ancient tongue,

"moon" and the word for deity in another—
I say it means the watch-glasses of your ankles,

or the wreaths of shadows around your eyes.
And some say a beloved's navel is a round goblet

and some, that it is the moon's drinking cup.
I say it is a mirror shining with reflections,

a receptacle for a clear wine, a centre
governing tides of life and death, creating time.

And I say your name keeps the first moonrise.
And I say your navel defines itself—

it is the sign of an invisible cord travelling
from beginning to beginning to beginning,

reminding me of everything as everything
reminds me of it, brimming beyond what I say.

Woolco

At the Woolco store where my mother worked
in the Red Grill, she was genuinely conscientious and efficient,

looking impressive and at the same time comical to us
in her red apron uniform and paper cap. The lipstick

and the touch of makeup she wore to hide her tiredness
only made her more of an attraction to the boss.

When she was on cash, she pretended not to know me
or any of my three younger brothers,

pretended to ring up the hamburgers and french fries
and milkshakes and sundaes we crammed onto our trays.

We loved Woolco. We walked almost proud out of the Red Grill
and spent my mom's shift investigating our favourite departments.

Sales clerks trained to be on the lookout for thieves
eyed us as we went up and down the aisles,

but my brothers and I still succeeded
in playing with much of the sporting equipment, riding bikes,

freeing motorized toy vehicles from packaging, trying on jackets.
At Christmastime, we deftly pulled the red hat from the head

of the Woolco Santa and his white hair and beard came off with it.
Later, we ran by him poking him in his red-velvet-clad belly.

Soon enough, they banned us from the roped-off Santa photo area.
It didn't matter. We brought our paint sets, Christmas presents

we knew our mom had lifted from a Woolco shelf
and hidden away in her bedroom closet. We would use them,

put them back in place and act surprised at Christmas.
We sat in the open area in the mall

and painted portraits of each of us sitting on the knee
of a hilariously grotesque Father Christmas. And of a beautiful cashier

with her name in ornate lettering on her name tag.
When the five of us piled onto the bus to go home,

the air was cold and tinselly as it began to snow,
and every block of the way the lights turned red, green, amber, red.

Memoir

In my memoir I will write about dust.
I will begin with the dust in the basement where I had my room.
I go down the stairs outside the old house
to the place below that is dark with dust.
During the day, I sweep the cement floor.
I sweep and try to stay ahead of the dust.
I shut and bolt the basement door from the inside.
I go half-frightened farther into the basement.
My room is off in the corner and has another door.
No matter how quickly I go to that door,
or how much I have swept, I cannot outrun the dust.
It deepens as I breathe it in, smell it, taste it.
I go to my room to dream, and can dream only of the dust
and how it has been here a long, long time
and how a thousand thousand things
flow into life from the dust.
I go back outside and am dust looking at dust.
The thousand thousand things are dust
that is concentrated, dust holding together as things.
The dust in the basement continues to deepen,
dead at the bottom of things.
In my memoir I will sweep and sweep the dust.
The earth pulverized before I was here,
the earth pounded invisibly to particles
that settle layer upon layer will fill me.
My memoir will be born in the dust.
If I mention love or loss, I will say how the source is dust.
If I see myself in a thousand thousand things,
I will say how I am a likeness.
There is too much dust for me to hold.
The narrative arc of my memoir

may owe something to me, to what I recall,
the dust may be me, but the dust forgets me,
it is too many things and holds too much more than me.
In my memoir I will say that as a young boy
I met the dust I will become when I die.
The basement is gone, my room gone,
that is why in my memoir I will begin here,
where the dust buries itself in dust, briefly sweet on the lips.

Coffee Cup Stain

A coffee cup stain—I see it
and think it must be from your cup.
Not that you really drank coffee—
one cup in the morning was it.
It's just that the stain is a ring,
a circle, here on a kitchen
surface usually wiped clean.

For two months now, I've been driving
around with them to and from work,
to and from my kids' school—bags full
of clothes in the hatch of my car;
I'm unable to bring myself
to drop them off at the thrift store.

Your Walmart wardrobe, your pairs
of budget shoes—I've carried them
within the routine of my days
and they've made a ring, and I want
the ring never to disappear,
but to stay as if it is you
still circling here through your own days,
the one who left a clear cup ring
that I simply happen to see.

You didn't drink coffee, really,
and toward the end, not even
that single cup in the morning—
though when you were in the hospice
I asked you if you'd like a sip.
You nodded and took a mouthful.
I love it, you said. *I love it.*

The Balmoral

Have you been incarcerated? a woman asked me,
startled at how pale I was.
I saw her and everyone else
spotlighted in the glare.
It was like a communal prison visit—
no touching across the tables,
no standing while holding a glass.
Beer seemed to be running
brilliantly through everyone's eyes.
The woman questioning me
was too smart for me.
My father hidden behind his beard
was too smart for me.
It felt like an initiation,
like I was there to undergo a kind of trial.
But he simply wanted me
to pay for his beer.
The glare was mechanical,
like a heavy electrical metal door
that a guard opened and shut.
The ordering of beer
was like a reciting of regulations.
It was like we were being filmed.
I was paying for my father's beer.
It's only time, he said.
I drank and paid and drank and paid.
I felt I might have died years before
according to some sentencing,
as my memory of myself
at eight or nine seemed to be all I was,
while he had existed

all along in a bright underworld
where he now laughed slyly
in my direction as he lifted
his glass to his lips, drinking time.

Blackouts

I was driving around in circles in the late evening
in a city on the east coast of the southern us.
The last thing I remembered was the sultry air
and the darkness flowing up out of the palm trees.
When I came to, it was morning. I was being pulled over
and directed back onto the highway. In a hotel bar
back in North Vancouver months later, I'd taken
only sips of a drink when I looked at who I was with
and realized I'd lost an hour. Something was broken
in my head from boyhood fights or childhood
beatings from my father, or a goblin within alcohol
was signalling my demise, or both, I didn't know.
Years later, blackness shouldered out of a brilliant
Greek afternoon from the far end of the light,
and I understood it was blackness through which light
was forever travelling. Light was evidence
a blackout was never only one kind of forgetting.
Light was travelling and becoming things
and was the way we see them. Light turned, continued,
and left a mirror behind. I had to clean it.
More years later, whatever I feel, light feels for me.
Light is beauty and is why we live our lives in arrears.
Light comes out of hiding to walk a street, a criminal
who can only be arrested, slip out of handcuffs,
and travel on, and we are gone. I must conduct
myself with dignity, however unwieldy. Blackness
compacts to make light as the light travels through it.
Withdraws from nowhere to become somewhere. Contracts
into a person who is barely here, and whatever
that person might create, he can never turn and see.
A gull gliding high beats its white wings once and cries

through the sky, and blocks out the sun, and the sun
reappears to count the same day again and again.

Light

I

There is light like falling rain,
like the first rain falling again,
like the first touch returning,
and arriving it meets light
here in the drift of two people
who lift to the face of the sun
now as if for the first time
to find the sun is a mirror
showing nothing but two people.

II

Touch here is clumsy, awkward,
and we go blind down dark roads,
sent out where light goes on ahead,
and take hands that hands can know,
while in the light waiting in us
there is no touch, one joins one,
and in that elsewhere the light
is like falling rain, like the first
and last rain and touch unfailing.

II

Voice

I

The dead can no longer hear,
and I can no longer remember
the sound of my heartbeat,
then hear it all around me in the rain.
The dead can no longer speak,
then their voices return,
none of them separate
from the rain repeating
it is no one, no one.

II

I want to gather up all distances,
rain whispering in my wrists,
breathing and reaching in my hands,
and murmuring in my marrow
which has always been the sleeper
who awakes within the bright
and measureless interior
of my own skeleton to turn
like rain to arriving rain.

III

Sometimes I hear the landline ring
and messages being recorded
a room away at odd hours,
and later nothing is on the machine.
It is my mother, who would usher us
out of our beds at night
to the open back door where
we would sit and listen. Wild rain,
she slips onto the porch of my ear.

IV

Psalms of the rain circling
in rhyming couplets, multiple
parallel repetitions, splashes,
countless collisions of rain
and the world's surfaces. Caesurae
vast as the absence
present in the mist arising
around the drops when rain
increases and fills its stillness.

V

Within the psalms a chant
that overwhelms words
to continue as touch on all
the skin at once, the syllables
echoing across the raindrops
like the visible and invisible
embracing in a single call,
the rain falls into the arms
of the first, unknown rain now.

An Old New Zealand Five-Pound Note

One of the two of them
who came looking for my mother
gave me an old New Zealand five-pound note
as a bribe to tell me where she was.
I had read a book about explorers
given to me by my father.
Captain Cook was my favourite,
and here he was on New Zealand money.
Where is she? he asked me, almost gentle.
I recognized him.
The other one, in a rugby jacket,
was becoming impatient.
I recognized him too.
She's in the Sandwich Islands, I said.
I thought the first one
got my little joke, as he then handed me
a handful of Canadian silver.
My mother was hiding
in the basement, which, in this old house,
was accessed from outside.
The first one was explaining to me
that the note would be valuable one day,
and that Cook had discovered
his country, New Zealand.
I told him that George Vancouver
had been a midshipman
in James Cook's crew
and had sailed into the inlet he could see
if he turned around and looked down the street.

They stepped into the front room.
My brothers were all asleep upstairs.
The impatient one pushed me.
I was too small to fight back.
My father, whom I would try to remember
as clearly as I could, was small too,
but I knew he would have dealt
easily with both these men.
He had always repeatedly hit
and kicked both my mother and me.
I looked down but still
kept my attention on the two men.
I was ten, and it was easy to pretend
to be a young boy.
I offered to show them around
the house and look for my mother
knowing they would never realize
she was in the basement.
I took them exploring
in errant directions until they gave up
on finding her
and went back where they had come from.
I kept the five-pound note in my book
about Captain Cook and the others
and would hold it up to the light
to see its line of gold thread
until years later when I left home
and all my old books were lost.

The Draftsman's Wound

A mechanical drafting set, circa 1960,
my grandfather's birthday gift to his son.
I open the black faux leather case. Inside,
green felt, drawing compasses, calipers
and dividers rarely if ever touched
in the decades since the son's twenty-first.
No instrument broken, each in its place,
the entire set is as the son left it
when he was instructed to take up tools,
limit, restrict and order, and that way
define himself complete. I bring each piece
of precisely finished aluminum
out into the light, note its name, function.
It is as if I have in front of me
a discovery of clean bone remains,
a single, wholly intact skeleton
laid in a case that is a lost coffin.
My father did not die but he began
to try to when this set was new. I see
how with equipment he finds on his own
to perform his now-necessary work,
he measures, marks off his distances,
executes his lines, divides his spaces.
I imagine how with his bones he draws
circle upon circle within himself.
If bones answer hands, the bones his hands move
allow him to make his final design.
He is dead now. I keep this drafting set
in its case as I might a set of bones,
and the bones reveal they are shining, fine,
incorruptible metal. With the bones

hidden in me, I hold my instruments.
My living hand, resembling his, will do
its different work, while the draftsman's wound
is unknown to me as it was to him,
and the bones of the father wound the son.

The Fraser Arms

I would go there to find him, once upon a time,
when the hotel was in its heyday.
He would look out from behind his glass
and tighten the outer corner of one eye,
his pause in his performance another performance.
A word or phrase or clipped anecdote
from any of his listeners, and he would interlace it
into the flow of his speech, his gestures.
He had said goodbye
to any history except what he created on the spot
and what was immediately a great archive
he then destroyed, sip by sip.
I would remind myself he was my father.
His performance rolled on.
People would sit around him, curious,
in the bar of the hotel
constructed thirty years before
on the site of the cleared away remains
of a Musqueam village.
Starting in the afternoon, he would hold forth.
His performance rolled on.
He would eye me from a distance.
I was just another person in an audience.
His performance rolled on.
People felt he knew something they didn't.
Closing time would come,
and he would still be there
at the location of the first
white settlement in Vancouver
on land that had been settled 4,000 years before.
Whatever had been handed down to him

he might have handed down to me, he had forsaken.
His performance rolled on.
There was no script, it was all improvised.
In another twenty years, the hotel would be gone,
the land would be reclaimed,
the nearby sawmill dismantled.
A son who had watched his father
fulfill his immigrant dream
of a house on the hill and Jaguars in the driveway
would be gone too,
improvising his way to an early death.
His performance rolled on.
There was no backstage, no dressing room,
no life offstage, and nowhere else
he existed but in the bar.
The was no curtain that would close
with a proper end, only a monologue
that rolled on and finally stopped.
The mirror behind the bar counter
consumed him and all that remained
was the picture I still have of him.
I see him there on the north bank
of the Fraser River, log booms edging
the back of the hotel property.
He's at the entrance,
ready to go to a nearby late-night restaurant
where he doesn't remember he's banned
for being a bad actor,
and the cab drivers are all aware of it
but take him anyway
for the last secret money
they know he has on him.

Shoes

Fire flew out the windows and laced up the building,
black smoke moved in mass after thick mass off the roof.
In one of the apartments was my mother.
She was old. She hardly understood.
Her eyes must have widened, while her pupils
must have constricted in the red and amber light.
Someone came to her door to escort her to safety.
White smoke drifted in a haze along the hallway ceiling,
strings of flame intertwined along the walls,
the air filled with the woofs of large unseen things igniting
as they rushed her to the stairwell and lobby exit,
and her eyes must have widened more and her memory
must have left her then as if a circuit breaker switch
had been flipped in her or a fire alarm lever had been pulled.
At the RCMP detachment evacuation centre
someone handed her a cell phone and helped her call me
and she told me she didn't have any shoes.
I could hear someone in the background explaining
home insurance, building repairs, reconstruction,
how it could take months, years, and she was telling me again
she didn't have shoes; she was without shoes.
Someone else was informing me where she was
because when I asked my mother, she didn't know,
all she knew was she wanted to go home.
The fire appeared then on my computer screen on the news,
the residents being ushered out to the street,
the fire trucks and men with helmets, gloves and hoses,
the ambulances and the police cars.
And I could have reported that my mother's eyes
must have widened more and her memory collapsed
like a flame-pushed ceiling, toppled like a flame-blasted wall,

and was taken up in swerving flame like the bush
that she set alight one day in the empty lot
beside the house where she lived when she was a girl,
her eyes widening before that fire, her life still ahead of her.
And on the phone she was telling me again
that she wanted to go home, and could I tell her the address,
as she had forgotten it, and could I bring her a pair of shoes.
I could see her building was mostly gone,
her address now the location of a fire, as I was to see
that during the same moments the conflagration
widened from its point of origin and her memory
fell away from her, the cancer that she had held
in abeyance must have relit itself, found its accelerant,
and metastasized, and her eyes widened more
because she was seeing within herself, while her pupils
turned to pinpoints before the fire of the cancer.
And when I arrived with borrowed shoes for her,
she was hardly my mother anymore,
and I felt I was hardly her son, I was a phone number
someone found for her on a piece of paper in her purse.
Still, she smiled at me and sat and put on the shoes,
repeating she wanted to return home, could I tell her the address,
and she stood up and was determined though the fire
had already burned her life down to a black and smouldering
and ruined foundation and shoes were unnecessary,
there was nowhere for her to go, and her only address
was displaying itself in her widening and changed eyes.

My Mother's Laughter

My mother laughed. When her first husband, my father,
battered her and burned her with cigarettes, soon enough she laughed.
When two men who had raped her returned to where she lived—

she and her four kids—and she hid, soon enough she laughed.
When she took me to see the latest lighthearted Hollywood movie,
she laughed hysterically, and no one in the theatre could hear anything

of the dialogue up on the silver screen, and she became the matinee.
When she finally attended one of my parent-teacher conferences,
trying to be serious about my schoolwork but failing, she laughed.

When she rode around the city on welfare day, her and her brood
the bane of a couple of bus drivers, my brothers and I
wrestling in the aisles and constantly ringing the buzzer, she laughed.

Before she could finish her own sentences, half the time she laughed.
Even when she cried, my mother laughed. If she cried
about some things, she cried tears of the laughing girl she had been

when she could not be called down from swinging atop tall trees
above all the houses, or when, a pregnant unwed mid-teen,
she insisted on parading me, her first to be, along the avenue.

If she cried about some things, she cried tears of the adult woman
within whom tears were converted to laughter
before anyone could see, even herself. It happened quick: she died,

and my mother took her laughter with her. Though not entirely,
as laughter that was hers is still echoing where she no longer is,
where we smile when we remember her and cry our tears.

My Father's Beard

My father's beard began as a moustache
when he was a married teen and a labourer for his father.
A year or two, and he wore a smart beard

that folded shadow like the metal he had to shear and rivet.
He let his beard grow. And his hair. His godhood grew in me,
and when I no longer saw him, I visualized him.

As soon as I could, I grew my own beard. I searched for him,
found where he lived and visited him in his floating home.
He had left his father's employ; I saw the work he did

in wrought iron with an air-hammer and acetylene torch—
tables, lamp stands, candle holders, wall decor, chandeliers.
His beard was Biblical, fierce and dark, beyond any other man's.

Half my life later, an instant in the timeline of ironwork—
in the history of the extraction of the ore from the earth,
the perfecting of smelting, purification, the fashioning of weaponry,

the creation of ornamental art, extending over millennia—
I saw him again and for a last time. His beard was silver, black-edged.
He lay in a hospital bed about to be wheeled to a morgue.

I do not remember ever having touched my father,
or him touching me except to strike me, but now I touched his beard.
It was the beard that had begun when I was small,

and had continued through the phases of his life,
and was now like a cathedral window screen or domestic grille,
or portal of intricate design. I could not stop there. I touched his face.

It was as if my hand met flesh of the first human dead,
and through my flesh, my own skeleton touched a skeleton—
and touched existence older than men. The beard remained his—

ironwork brought to a fine elaboration, the artistry complete,
ore transformed, set in place, opening on what was invisible,
yet leading back again to every beginning in the dark earth.

Ruin

His tiny one-room apartment is a ruin.
The bookcase, table, chair and bed, which he made, are falling apart.

The companion bird that flew free around the room,
and one night writhed on the floor as he watched, or dreamt he watched,

unable to move from his bed to help—that bird's old excrement
along with the bird seed he scattered for it is everywhere.

The books are musty, crusted. The brass pieces, covered in dust.
The bird was never seen again. It might have made its way, he said,

out the window to chirp to the dawn and die—while he slept.
In the room where he ended up, light reached the bed

through the clean glass and fell across the general whiteness,
but in his apartment—which will now have to be cleared out,

his possessions disposed of or given away—light falls across a ruin.
I take half a dozen books, a brass vase—

mementos of my father, whom I have not seen
since I was a young man. I am collecting antiquities.

In the room where he ended up, the daylight found him, found the sheets,
the pillows, the medical machinery set up at his bedside,

but that light could never be as new as the light falling
across the room where he lived as across an ancient site

and across crumbling furniture, forms collapsing brightly from within,
never as new as the light returning here, refining itself

and continuing his fate where time has made a ruin,
the morning beginning again and beginning before all his mornings.

Nightstand

Sanding a small nightstand
come down to me from my father,
removing dents and abrasions,
taking away the old finish,
beginning a final smoothing,
I go back to the origin
of the piece—from the tongue
and groove to the glueing up
of the panels and the clamping,
from the cutting to the marking
with a knife, to the measuring.
I sand until the hands at work
with finer and finer grades
of grit show me his hands and I see
the man I saw fleetingly
in his life examining the wood
and imagining the nightstand,
its simple lines, its single drawer.
I sand and follow the grain
to where he falls away,
then immediately further back
to where he is briefly a father,
young and hampered and cruel,
and briefly a laughing mid-teen,
and finally, a lonely child.
I smooth the wood surface more,
and he is no longer there,
and although I am not him,
I turn and know the route
he found within and had to take
to meet himself and meet no one.

Throughout a morning, I restore
the piece my father prepared
in the presence of passing time,
and I anoint the wood with oil
and let it dwell where I live
so that I can keep in my days
what I have of what he made.

Gesture

On my way out of his room
I said, *I'll see you.* He raised his arm.
I didn't think he had the strength.
His forearm straight up, his knuckles
facing me, he pumped his fist,

bright, bitter glory in his eyes.
Was it an insult? Was it pride
flaming in him even when he lay
immobile, loose, fleshless skin
hanging from arm and leg bones?

I didn't know. I half-smiled at him
and left, feeling what I realized
a moment later was hope.
That I meant something to him.
That he had signalled me, *Go on*

in the fight of life. He was a day
away from death. Perhaps the gesture
was meant to oblige; I was his son.
But perhaps meant as more. Perhaps.
I took that. I took what I could

of the certainty of his love. I held on
to it as a last communication
from my father. He had been gone
and I had become a yearning boy.
His ashes are buried in my arm.

III

A Dance

When you did that quick dance in the doorway
in your t-shirt, hair thrown back, hands flung up,
I knew I had always been left behind.

You were burning; burning, you blinded me;
I knew I had been blinded from the start,
when you did that quick dance in the doorway.

You turned, you smiled, and I thanked the power
you knew was moving with you as you moved;
I knew I had always been left behind.

I watched, and my watching was my burning;
my eyes threw me in the fire where you burned,
when you did that quick dance in the doorway.

In that instant, I lived the entirety
of my visit here, and I followed you;
I knew I had always been left behind.

My only light my being blind, I stood
burning and suddenly knew who I was
when you did that quick dance in the doorway;
I knew I had always been left behind.

Shawl

You drew a shawl of woollen yarn around your shoulders. In a room in your mother's house, you took the ends of the shawl in your fingertips and brought it across yourself. The spun sheep's wool stretched, the loose knit of the shawl opened circles across you, the shawl covered you. I took your hands. You held my hands and spread out our arms in a circle.

While you had looked for me, I had looked for you. I walked until there was no longer a city, no street other than your street, and I was like dust a slow wind was carrying along that street. I came into your mother's house under the archways of your eyes.

The knit of the shawl caught the dawn light coming through a window. The light became one with the turns of the yarn. It seemed in that moment you spun the yarn and knitted the shawl.

I pulled the shawl away. It slipped to the floor. I pushed away a part of the cotton blouse that lay lightly over your shoulders. I did this gently. Even so, I knew I could only bruise you. Your shoulders of white wine. Your shoulders still brushed with the blackness of the night. Light fell across the canopy of your eyelashes. It travelled the twists and loops of your hair. And I blinded my eyes.

I left your mother's house. I made my way back to the city streets. A police vehicle stopped alongside me. The officers took me into custody. They seemed to know me. I understood little of the language in which they questioned me.

I lay on a cold ledge. The room was windowless. I did not know when they would release me. But I knew the knit of the shawl was a touch. You drew the shawl around your shoulders. You allowed the knit of the shawl to take me in. Everything within you was knitting the shawl, a touch within a touch. Light was coming forth across a far-off field.

Hibiscus

my sister, my spouse…
—Song of Songs 4:10

In the picture you paint of a hibiscus,
you reveal yourself in a glossy red flower.

The corolla accomplishes its whorl
and flows into the invisible though it is still here—

the invisible rushes into the petals.
My sister, my spouse… Now an address manifests

as the filaments and anthers of the stamen
the full flower gathers and gathers in.

Petals part to display the pads of the stigma;
the petal-circle of sight is complete;

the pistil collects pollen from the air,
allows it down the inside of the style

to the ovary older than any flower's fading—
in the picture you make. Your trumpet-shaped,

large-petalled hibiscus blooms where the light
can go no farther before it is lost

and finds a way through you back to a sun,
its corolla, its petals' endless smile.

Prophecy

I have eaten my honeycomb with my honey…
—Song of Songs 5:1

"You are the colour of honey," your mother said to you
when you were newly born and lay against her breast—

words I would later repeat, uttering a directive
to wait like a drone bee at the bee nest

where the hexagonal prismatic cells
hidden within the thicket hold honey.

They say the star inside the hexagon
contains the forms of the invisible body of love,

and with the sound of their vibrating wings,
their low singing, honeybees spin sunlight.

They say the veil-wings of the queen bee block the sun
to allow a drone bee to pass through other veils

into an inner sanctum where a secret light is stored.
I see atoms in the human egg flash as it is fertilized.

I see my task must be to wait to fall away
in the honey of the moment when you are here, here, here,

and be restored again, fulfill a prophecy—
I have eaten my honeycomb with my honey.

Henna

Let us go out into the fields
and lie all night among the flowering henna…
—Song of Songs 7:12

You leave henna in your hair for the night,
as you do every month; now the scent has lain down with us,

and I have come to think it is henna
you have used to colour the nails of your fingers and feet,

and now your menstrual blood stains the sheet a shining red,
and its scent is that of the summer sun

that has lain all day in an ancient field of long grass—
the scent releases itself from your hair

and rolls from you, another body, and another you.
You take up the sheet, I take up the sheet with you;

we wrap it around ourselves like a garment dyed scarlet—
a single henna shrub is thriving here with us.

The scent arrives and arrives from out of the roots,
leaves and white blossoms of a flowering plant

arriving more fully than if we could see it,
and continuing more subtly than if we could tend to it;

it makes its own way through us, and is another body
turning within us while we sleep and while we wake.

Names

... our bed is green.
The beams of our house are cedar,
and our rafters of fir.
—Song of Songs 1:16–17

I count backward through the beams and rafters
of our house and through the unfinished wood base of the bed—

through beams of cedar and rafters of fir
and through a platform and piled boughs to living trees.

I count backward through the bundles of spiralling,
lengthening needle-like leaves to the many trees

under the sky drinking the rain of the air,
under the forest floor interlacing in dark meeting places

and drinking the waters of the earth through their roots.
I count backward through a rough bedchamber

with a canopy of branches, a screen of fronds, to two people
twining within a green eye that begins with them

and opens for them to find what they do not know
of each other where all numbers and all letters are green,

where they are guilty but only of paradise,
its naming of them while they lie in a green bed,

beneath them the laid-out boughs, above them
the beams and rafters of all names saying *I am.*

The Field

I was standing near a field.
I felt I had stood somewhere like this before,
but could not remember. It was completely dark,
no city lights, and almost dawn.
I sensed long green grass, wildflowers,
multicoloured insects, small birds.

At the edge of the field was a woman.
She turned and looked at me.
She threw something to me.
I caught it and immediately threw it back to her.
She let the thing fly past her into the field.

I went into the field to find it.
The sun had risen. I could see a crater
where a cluster bomb had been dropped,
heaped dirt and sand, black ash,
shell holes, shell casings, flechettes.

The field had been scorched but was now cold.
Artillery and gunfire, round after round,
finally, a blast wave, had been all of sound.
But the field was now silent.

In the middle of the field lay a sphere
the size of a pumpkin or a classroom globe.
I went close. I saw the sphere was a mine—
not an anti-tank or anti-personnel mine,
but a type once deployed
in secret locations in bodies of water.
I could see the mine's detonator horns.
It was out of place in this field.

Beside the mine lay the thing
the woman had thrown to me, and I had thrown to her,
and she had then let land in the field.
The thing looked the same as the mine.
Now that light was filling the field,
the thing shone like a golden ball.

I picked the thing up and threw it
back out of the field to the woman.
The woman caught it this time.
She simply looked at me again, expressionless.
She threw the thing back into the field.

The thing lay at my feet again.
Again, I bent to pick it up. The instant I did this,
I could no longer see the field,
but felt I had been dispersed with great energy
and was present in every particle holding
the value of the field in space and time.
I did not know what field I had become,
but I had become everything in the field.

Snow

When snow lulls you and does away with distances,
you fall to the circular margin of yourself,

look within the circle, know you are gone—
there at the level of the lost earth is a site

of stones and ancient dust where little grows
but intermittent tufts of awed, wild grass.

Here too it has begun to snow lightly
where it rarely snows, and snow is a wheel

of flakes that can move in all directions
arriving at hill after waiting hill.

Once, it was too far for you to travel
to this murmuring ground, this radial city,

but news of it reaches through you now undelayed
as water scarce in this place but lifting

with all water into the upper air and descending
carries in its changed, elaborately dead arms

of ice crystal the unknown, the designing cold.
And the wheel of the snow spins and lays down

beyond measuring by centimetre
or light-year the flakes that make the night bright,

the lattices of hexagonal rings
that were you before you were you, and allow you

to be you, vanish the way they vanish,
story upon story once told, again untold.

The Name of the Creek

In the waters' quick pulsebeat flow, the creek carries its name
from the source to the mouth, carrying it down the mountain
and down through the glacial till to the inlet.
It is summer now and the waters run lit and light green
and run shallow and smooth and laced with fine white froth.
It is winter now and the waters run dark grey
and run deep and wild and tufted with whitewater
and continue rhythmic and calm. It is spring now
and the waters rise with the snowmelt as they rose with melting ice
thousands of years ago and carried the creek's name.
Now the creek carries the low clouds of its valley,
the air of its narrow, sheer-walled canyon and travelling fine mist,
carries jutting rocks, crowds of boulders in its flow,
carries clay down from its banks to the mouth.
Salmon journeying up the creek carry its name
leaping ripple after ripple, swirling in eddies, and spasming
in high pools, and carry it until they die in those pools,
salmon newly born carry it flitting down to the inlet and the sea.
Herons come up the creek lifting away, standing still and lifting away,
and carry the name within the alphabet of their wings
that open and span the countless characters of the creek
all tumbling over each other and still spelling the name.
When the days of rain feed the unknown source,
clappers strike sound bows of bells throughout the creek
to ring the name, and when rain falls into the entire creek,
the rocks and boulders hum the name, and the name deepens in the flow.
All this time, the creek collects and collects its name,
its name becomes water, is lost, found and lost again in water,
it says its name and its current swerves through the name.
All the time I have been able, I have said the name of the creek,
but only the name I learned as a child, and to show I had learned it

I repeated it on a morning when my father visited
and he and I walked the length of the gravel of the creekside trail.
Like the many who said it, I said a name for the creek
that was not the name that had been shared down through the millennia
alongside the light green and dark grey and white-fringed waters
among the ones who created paths here after the ice melted
and the waters first surged and reached from the source to the mouth.
Although I was born not far from the creek, I did not know that name.
I know now that name was lost, but I can read it,
I can sound it out: Ha-ul-cha. I can say it, and hear the name
flowing and singing as it always has beneath the name Lynn Creek.
It is a gathering of sounds passed down from mouth to ear to mouth,
it is the name the creek flows through all at once: Ha-ul-cha.
It is just a name. It has no meaning, an Elder said to me.
The name of the creek has no meaning; the name arrives and arrives
as the creek arrives and arrives and arrives and arrives,
and only the creek can say its name, which will always mean nothing.
No name for the creek can say more than the flowing waters,
no waters say more than the name no one can know.

Mist

It is mostly emptiness, and at this instant it is all I can see,
water droplets suspended like a shining mask.

The world is primarily emptiness, it is said,
and if all matter were compacted, it would fill

only a single human being. And even then, matter
would continue to reveal it only tends to exist.

Here all matter is mist. I believe the mist forms from all
the people I have known, all I will never know,

and all I meet in dreams but are unfamiliar to me,
following its designs through their every affinity.

A couple interlaces arms, mostly emptiness
stretching farther than they know; they switch back and forth

the same mask of mist for their untraceable faces.
It is always bright behind their eyes; darkness they disguise

is always a form of light. Here the mist hides a white sun
out on an ocean. Here the sun displays itself

within a human being like a mirror. In this mirror,
the reflection looking back is always a mask;

the mirror is mirror after mirror after mirror.
It is all I can see, warm vapour arriving suddenly

at the only place it can arrive, meeting the cold shore,
coming into the world, beginning again, becoming mist.

Delivery

Beyond the adorning of a ceremonial dress
is the continual hands taking hands

to carry things old, new, borrowed and blue—
a blind animal of rhythm and swerve;

a seed, a dying flower and the plant's time-lapse;
a cast, a mould, a melting, a cooling—a chiselling away

revealing the original contours of the bronze;
a filling cup, a breaking cup, a waiting cup.

No guests, no witnesses, except the two of them—
they are there; still, they cannot turn and see themselves

as they are carried where they need to go. They know
the end of what they can see will make them no one.

What arrives with them invents them, they invent it,
and they are taken across and across

the dark that is always ahead of them,
and what arrives with them is what delivers them

into the day made of lovers travelling to lovers,
where they will cry the light like a newborn.

Summer Morning

The tree is young, far younger than the light
it is flinging up out of its trunk and curved limbs

like an offering. And the tree is old, as old
as lovers who forgot their own histories long ago.

The light turned within the tree as it rose,
the way the two turned within each other. The one

who would never go from this place even after
the love failed, and survived long after the other

left and lived a life elsewhere and died,
is still desiring, still lifting light up out of the earth

that is made of nothing except the love.
The light fills the branches, the twigs, and in the air

around the leaves, where it is still meeting
the sunlight plunging to it, it is all a white melting.

The leaves will fall as if throwing themselves
onto a pyre where a beloved lies, and touch cold ground,

but now the light begins, it seems it will never end,
and the earth begins again, beginning to burn.

Hummingbird in that Second

In that second, the hummingbird
is a green electron in two places simultaneously,
a glass of green liquor brewed millennia ago,
a miniature green time machine,
a fistful of purple-green air before thunder,
a green moon orbiting almost too quickly for us to see,
a light taking the hand of the green
of my grandmother's irises in a dance as grave as it is joyous.
In that second, it is a single syllable
ushering in all the greenness of the planet,
and is gone, leaving all syllables, all words,
all wanting to be that single syllable again.

In that second, the hummingbird
perches on the twig of a small tree in the rain
and keeps the pathway it travels from here to Chile and back
through forest-fire-scorched California
within its body like folded-up space,
and with raindrops arriving in sequence like a string of numbers,
is in mid-air again in its courtship dive,
beating its wings two hundred and sixteen times,
the sum of the numerical values
of the letters in the seventy-two hidden names of God,
the code for the first matter the mist
sweeping around it, in that second.

IV

Play Structure

A play structure is collecting children. A multiple combining of atoms is occurring. My alphabet, my wristwatch hour, collapse as kindergarteners exit school to go quickly to fulfill the formula for the molecule of molecules. They do not know the molecule frees them from the custody centres of their classrooms with the help of their waiting smiles and shouts. The light alive within the molecule pays the bail and supervises the probation. The light puts on masks and performs each child. A child is a symbol of a child. They do not know they run and propel the plot of the light. Light assigns roles in a numberless cast demanding heroism of breath act after act. They do not know, as they circle, their smiles and shouts are dialogue, are speeches, are an ongoing series of letters, epistles of many hands. The electrostatic attraction between atoms is allowing the molecule to compose itself: light is writing to light. They do not know that together they sign a chemical signature. That signature is impossible to read, it is secret, it forms too fast, completes its flourish, and erases itself too fast. I see the play structure is a molecule of children, I see it is the way light discovers its origins. Light writes to children and children write back, and the content of any of the letters is light and is immediately the postscript of light, yet the child I follow with my eyes is also my daughter whom I named and who runs and plays with her friends.

Peter's Ice Cream

Surprise heat. I don't remember
it ever being so hot
at this time of year,
the sun so strangely bright.
I know that as my memory
takes in more and more of my dead,
the light hitting my eyes
increases, intensifies.
Suddenly—my mother
and lemon ice cream.
And my father. It's the time
I went with them to Peter's,
the array of flavours
in front of us behind glass
like a full spectrum
including all the colours
I couldn't normally see.
I watch the two of them
choose the same flavour—
not ice cream but sherbet.
They're exquisitely young,
barely out of their teens,
but they're a couple, and happy.
I don't see the flavour
I decide on for my own cone—
it's my memory's secret,
though it's what I most truly know
and is the treat of my life
that time shares with me.
It's out of place here,
this heavy, severe light,

and it's impossible—
my mother and father alive,
the three of us together,
and colour a flavour we choose
before colour's tipping point,
before a final signalling
that the world is about to burn.
The first day of the summer
that we'd have gone to Peter's
and stood in the warmth and sparkle
will dawn under a heat dome.
I look back, look back again,
and whatever I try to see
announces a beginning
beyond my seeing,
but that changes, and all there is
is like an ending now—
it's here in the trapped fiery air,
it's what we share and dream
will always outlast us,
and is our only spring.

Note on My Father and Alchemy

To wait for spring
is to remember the year plant leaves
opened strangely early

like a lion's mouth to eat the sun
and create new greenness.
I shaded my eyes—

I looked for him, and found
a killing acid dissolving
metals into their beginnings,

releasing green madness,
and I was condemned
to be without his love.

Now he is the essence of memory,
now light I hope to see.
The lion's jaws open

and in the emptiness
displaying itself in the mouth,
love knows to wait

for light to arrive
from the burning gases of the sun.
That interval

is the spring day
on which I must tame
the sudden darkness within me.

Let the green lion
of my love eat the sun, be living gold,
and me be made of that love.

Power

The power goes out with a quiet click,
and for a moment I forget where I am,
then I think I must have missed this month's bill payment,
then that it's my mother, who departed a year ago
or a lifetime ago, or possibly my deceased father
communicating with me from the beyond.

Then I step outside and see the others
standing in front of their own doorways, and I know the electricity
has failed throughout the complex.
The windstorm that blasted the last leaves from the trees
and flung them like bits of rusted chain to doorsteps
likely brought down lines across the city.

Everyone is outside now. The lamplight
of the living rooms behind them gone,
the screens black and empty, the pictures named and arranged
on the bedroom walls disappeared in the darkness,
the kitchen calendars dissolved,
all the rooms suddenly soundless.

I don't know any of them. I've lived here with my family a year
but have never said hello to a neighbour.
Ours is always the first to go out, I hear one say,
and always the last to come back on.
I see they're used to this, and they'll simply
stand here and wait like inmates for a count.

I can't help it; I think this is it, the end of things,
and the power won't come back on,
and it was stupid of me to believe we could fill
these spaces with ourselves, our belongings and memories,
and mark off our days here and call it home.
The rooms we inhabit seem replicas of rooms.

I realize I will have to leave, and go look for kindling
and pieces of wood to make a fire, though I hardly know how,
and be afraid I will burn my hands,
and the firelight hurt my eyes. Out in the elsewhere
of the night, the hours until the rising
of the original sun will be like a long journey.

Already, I know that when I come back
I will be blind to much of what I always thought was real,
and when I rejoin those who stayed, found new shadows,
my wife and child among them, I will be afraid,
unable now to see the ones closest to me
here with what is bright and invisible and true.

Level

Water will find its level and spirit find it as well.
I see my mother, her life in the flesh over,

continually seeking her own level around me.
The trees drawing water up into the leaves of the sky,

the grass leaning like a wave, the deep pools
in the river canyon turning clearer and clearer green,

the rain running downhill like a wild child in the creek—
it is all coming into my eyes and is her

and she is almost finding herself here again.
Or it is me, and I am walking at the level of my eyes

in water that has been here before, and was here always,
and coming from within me to meet what I see—

it is a subtle flood carrying me, not drowning me
but wrapping around me and holding me complete

as within womb water about to break.
And water will go on discovering confines,

water itself a confine of light, and light free itself,
become water again circling through eyes,

and my mother find her level here fleetingly as me,
exactly as water would have me tell.

A Corpse

Here is his corpse in a hospital bed—
the soft, silver-white hair falling to the shoulders,
the flesh thin on the high cheekbones, the skull a throne,
the nose high-bridged and long, the old beard long,
the half-exposed, shrunken body stiffening,
the organs within it still as stone, the skeleton a throne.
The curtain drawn in the acute care room
where he died three hours ago. The mouth open,
the round abyss of a gasp, the eyes open,
no longer blue, dark grey, stopped up as stone,
and unyielding, contained in a new aloneness.
What I am that he was, I owe to the desire
that was like an edict in a solitary,
wild young man and a smiling young woman
summoning me from an elsewhere into the flesh.
I take the sheet edge, cover, tuck him in,
and wait for the aides to come to wheel him away.
I wait as when I was a child waiting months, years
to see him, my father, my absent king.
I see him step down from his elevated sitting place,
put on armour, wield weaponry like any man.
I tend to him as I would tend to a soldier,
light waning over a now-quiet field where he lies dead.
I advanced alongside him like a brother, I saw him fall.
I sit with him so that he will not be alone,
and I guard him, guarding my truest self,
until the air around me is dark, and I go.

A Coat

Found in a storage locker and passed on to me:
his flamboyant coat. Canvas with bands of varying shades of beige,

fur-lined, canvas belt, cast-iron buckle. I try it on.
I remember seeing him from a cab I was driving—

wearing it while he sold drugs. Now it is my coat
of many colours, his unintentional gift to me.

His seed travelled this far; his DNA arrays the large pockets
fringed in elaborate embroidery, red, yellow, blue.

He could never have known I would fall on my own
into a pit or dip myself in my blood to prove I could die,

try to become him, the unfathomable source
of the visible spectrum of the judgement he brought down.

Or that I would chase blackness—all colours receding before me—
after he vanished into jail then into dark streets.

My Egypt was my being his eldest and not his youngest son,
recognized, mistaken as him, hated by the others,

and costuming myself in clothes like his to cover bones.
I learned earliest how inheritance meant prison stripes.

Now it is my coat, but it was always my coat.
Now if I wear it, I wear it as myself, my father, brothers,

all of us warm, fed, unindebted, then as none of us,
the colours all the coat that light can wear.

They Wheel Me

They lose their memories in front of me,
my grandparents, my mother, my aunt,
they fall away until they are only the light
of their now haggard eyes,
their eyes that recognize me
though they may forget my name
or our exact familial connection.
Here, I say, pointing to a calendar,
is the day, month, year. Here are photos
of you when you were young,
of your parents, your old house. Here
is you driving my brothers and me
in your car. Here is a fresh cup of tea.
It is always their last summer.
I wheel them over uneven sidewalks.
I wheel them up and down curbs.
They note new buildings, new stores.
They repeat, it is wonderful to be outside.
They squint in the sun.
They do not remember
when they were last outside—
though they were the week before,
the week before that...
They pushed me in a small stroller once—
which I cannot remember.
They applauded when I took my first steps.
And they wheel me now.
I wheel them, I catch the sun
in the wheels of their chairs,
and time circles around and around—
days wondering about days,

hours thinking about hours,
years meditating on years:
I see their recollections flash
in the spinning silver spokes.
And they wheel me
as they go in their chairs where time goes,
and it takes me,
as they go where time attends time
and is light, and it takes me.

Streets of Snow

I

Snow was falling on already fallen and frozen snow
and we went out to it as if to meet and welcome it
and as if we had been instructed to do so.
The far-flung, empty streets, already white,
were becoming whiter and beginning to sparkle,
and the spaces within the snowflakes were absorbing sound
and everywhere was quiet like the interior of a temple,
the snowdrifts like the walls of a temple.
You adjusted your wool scarf as a chill went through you,
and I wrapped the scarf more completely around you
and you swept away the snowflakes from the fleece
of your hair that came down out of your wool hat
and you held your eyes closed for a moment
to melt the snowflakes caught on your eyelashes,
yet the snow as soon swirled around and covered you again
like a linen dress, a wide, glittering necklace,
ornaments, and an elaborate veil, and it was light falling,
filling the spaces within the crystals of the snowflakes.

II

And snow was falling all the time concealing light
and revealing it as in a consummation, a longed-for act,
and the light arrived and I reached into the snow
pillowed along a handrail as I might reach for a ring of light
that the snow had designed to put your finger through,
but found darkness was on the other side of each snowflake.
And the day turned to evening, and I touched fingers
of darkness with fingers that were themselves darkness
in those streets of snow, and I saw the snow that adorned you
had melted under the canopy of snow clouds
and your dress had fallen away, and you now wore a cloak
of darkness and you were confounded and lost, and the light
that had come forth within the snow was gone.
Like the snow you could only relinquish rescue,
and when the snow stopped and melted then froze,
you walked again in the forlornness of those streets,
and when the darkness released you again,
you lifted your eyes' wreaths of shadows to that beginning.

Story

Biblical downpour. An atmospheric river
from out over the heat-pushed Pacific,
carrying as much water as any earthbound river,
hurrying to the coast range
and letting fall more rain in a day
than any total ever of a handful of days.
Hour by hour it continues,
it is unstoppable
and is every timeless story
remembered and then forgotten again
where it floods into the reported news.
Right now, all roads washed out,
fields under the flow, milk cows
dragged off, drowned, houses
pulled from foundations, overturned, sunk.
If I say two by two
go to be saved, it is no me or you,
only a single
other within the familiar river
travelling fast, unconfined,
and free to drag the muck of memory away.
Whatever heaven we dreamt
spends its energy
along with whatever life we ruined,
as high as any riverside
and as low as any riverbed.
When the rain lessens
and the waters recede,
rain simply gathers in a circle in lit air
around evacuees
who return, who are their only ark,

and who sit on mysterious ground
looking up through a gentle shower
at the sun as at a storyteller
until they start to forget
all they believed was true.
When rivers of fire rain down, it will be the same;
there has never been anywhere
to go but the rain.

The White Light of Tomorrow

Now overpowering sunlight.
Father, I will look for you always.

From under my brow, which is your brow.
Through the eye's metal, madness in the sun

and your hidden elation.
All the dead—

darkness, a way; light, every place.
Light turns here and is a person.

Memory is a hold
on who I am and is locked up in matter.

The spring sun melts
my future at the heart of metal.

In the gap between a ray
of light leaving the sun and arriving at my eye,

my life halts. Immediately behind it
darkness opens, and what is being born

is far away, and I look for it
as I look for you, father.

A long, narrow way leads within me
and out again in a circle. There is no tracing

any ray back to the moment it left the sun.
The entire sun abandons darkness in each ray.

Light, my fate.
Love, my memory of light.

All that goes by my brow—the invisible
concentrating into the visible

and on its way elsewhere.
Light on its way through darkness to you, father.

Colour

The eye apparels the world in colour,
but the eye shops mass-market retail. That is why when you
turn down a clothing aisle you walk into your only dream wardrobe,
and why you ask a sales associate for her ring of keys
and try on the maximum of the same three articles again and again.
The eye is paint-by-number. That is why when you
hire an art model and she arrives at the studio of your eye's pupil
and you ask her to disrobe, and you notice the discolourations
riddling her flesh, the scars, and the amount of makeup
on her ravaged face, you take up your brush and dress her
in the colours of a dog walker along a lawn-lined street.
And the eye is death. That is why the star that is the sun
and all colours supplies millions upon millions of product runs.
That is why whoever you walk with in the sun,
you see in colours that repeatedly go black like a dead sun,
though you want to believe you have beheld her in all her colours
and nothing of what you feel for her has been a pretense.
Both her death and yours are visible directly
in front of you, where you aim and click your eye's price-tag gun
and apply your bar codes to the colourless welter.
You forget your death, but it waits in a changing room
with every piece of clothing you have tried on, or will try on.
You remember your death, and your death forgets you,
and if the eye of love looks through your eye at another,
colour flows, leans toward you though only as it curves away.

Notes & Acknowledgements

The title of this collection is taken from a passage in the poem "The Far Field" by Theodore Roethke:

> *I learned not to fear infinity,*
> *The far field, the windy cliffs of forever,*
> *The dying of time in the white light of tomorrow,*
> *The wheel turning away from itself,*
> *The sprawl of the wave,*
> *The on-coming water.*

Many thanks to the editors of the magazines in which some of the poems in this book (one or two in earlier versions) first appeared:

Event—"Moon"; "Note on My Father and Alchemy";
  "A Coat"; "Snow"
The Fiddlehead—"Nightstand"
Grain—"The Name of the Creek"; "The Field"
Juniper—"Hummingbird in that Second"
The Malahat Review—"Play Structure"
Prairie Fire—"Names"
Vallum—"Gesture"

An earlier version of "Henna" appeared in the collection *The Fifth Window* (Thistledown Press, 2000).

Many thanks to everyone at Harbour Publishing. And many thanks to Silas White for his editing.

*A masterful new collection from
award-winning poet Russell Thornton.*

The White Light of Tomorrow showcases a poet of intense lyricism and
distinctive imagination. The pieces in this collection enact a compelling
visionary movement between the substance of water, where the poet
wakes to "the aloneness of water," and the phenomenon of light, where
he comprehends "light" as "fate" and "love" as "memory of light." Along
the way, with originality and highly affecting depth of feeling, Russell
Thornton explores elemental themes of romantic and familial love, death,
grief, memory, and beauty.

Passionate and moving, *The White Light of Tomorrow* marks an impressive
advance in Thornton's expanding poetic output.

HARBOUR PUBLISHING

www.harbourpublishing.com
Ebook also available
Printed in Canada

ISBN 978-1-990776-53-3

9 781990 776533

51895

22.95 CAD / 18.95 USD

Guard bees protect the hive. If a hornet, bumblebee, or any other creature tries to get in, the guard bees sting them! The scent of the sting's venom warns all the bees in the hive about the intruder.

This wasp spider works hard to weave
its web between the branches of a bush.
It makes spider silk in a special organ called
a spinneret. Some of the silk released from its
abdomen is sticky, and the spider knows how to tiptoe
around its web to keep away from the sticky parts.

The spider can't see very well, but it can feel its web move. As it creeps over to its prey, the spider injects the cricket with venom, keeping it from moving, then wraps it in silk. The spider will feast on the cricket later. Meanwhile, it keeps a watchful eye on the bird on a nearby branch. It does not want to be the bird's meal!

A female common yellow swallowtail butterfly has laid a tiny egg on a twig. A week later, a caterpillar hatches out of the egg, and it is hungry. It eats up the egg case, as well as the nearby leaves.

It keeps eating and grows fast!

About 10 days later,
a full-grown butterfly
comes out of the chrysalis.

A few weeks later, it releases a
thread of silk to attach itself to the
stem of a plant. Then after shedding
its skin one last time, it forms a
chrysalis around itself.

Ready to fly, the swallowtail flaps its wings a few times before letting the wind carry it into the air. The butterfly glides like a kite, then stops to gather food.

Flitting from flower to flower, it uses a long, thin tube called a proboscis to suck up nectar, its favorite food.

On the forest floor, ants gather materials for their home.
Each ant carries a twig or pine needle between its jaws.

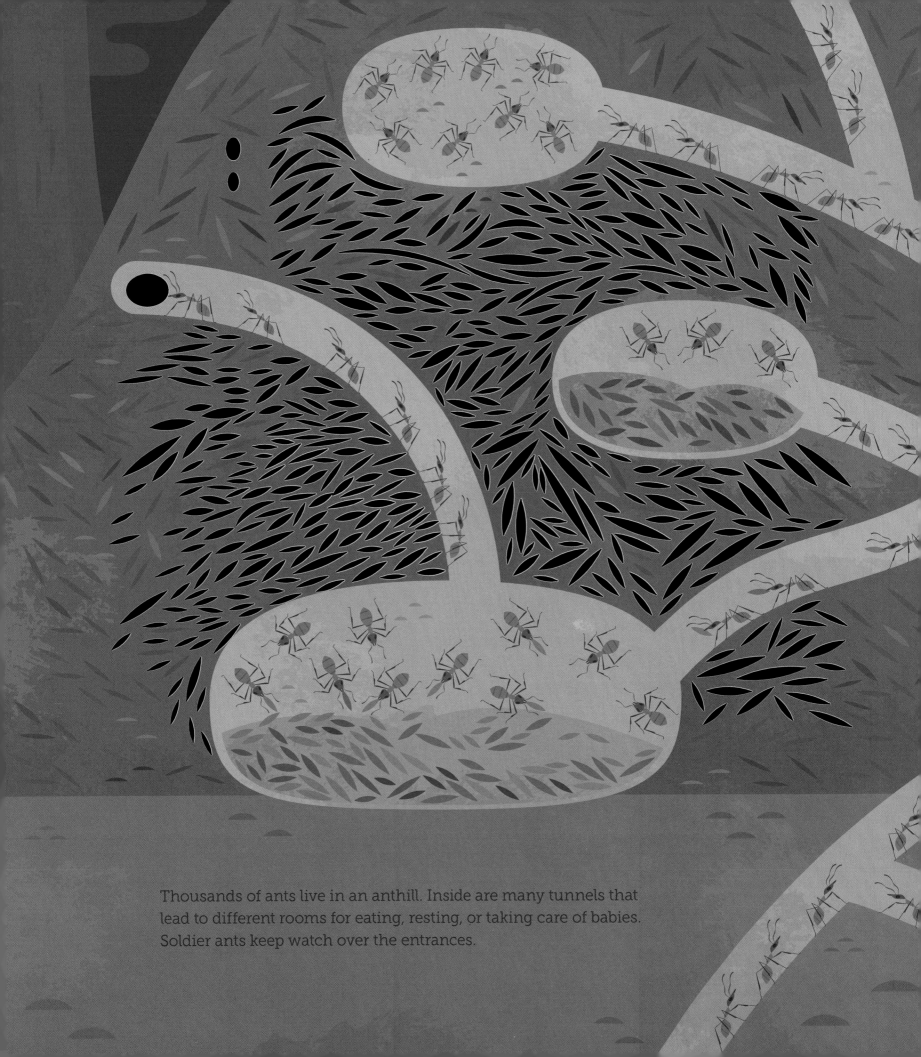

Thousands of ants live in an anthill. Inside are many tunnels that lead to different rooms for eating, resting, or taking care of babies. Soldier ants keep watch over the entrances.

Besides soldier ants, there are workers, builders, and nurses. They work all day around a single large queen ant, who is the only one who lays eggs.

What beautiful colors! The wings of the damselflies sparkle in the sun. Damselflies live close to ponds, pools, and other bodies of water. They feed on flies, mosquitoes, and beetles.

Male damselflies have blue wings, while female damselflies have golden wings. When they are resting, damselflies hold their wings upright, above their bodies.

Their legs have bristly hairs that are used
to perch on plants—or capture prey!

The birds and lizard are looking for bugs to eat. They don't seem to notice that the twig-like creatures on the plant stems are stick insects, which stay very still to avoid being spotted.

When night falls, the birds and lizard are gone, and the stick insects become more active. They move carefully, nibbling on plants and leaves.

When they sense danger, the stick insects stretch out their front legs and freeze. Their sticky back feet allow them to hold this position for a long time. The insects can even fall to the ground and play dead!